Book 1
C++ Programming Professional
Made Easy

BY SAM KEY

&

Book 2
Ruby Programming
Professional Made Easy

BY SAM KEY

Book 1
C++ Programming Professional Made Easy

BY SAM KEY

Expert C++ Programming Language Success in a Day for Any Computer User!

Programming Box Set #59: C++ Programming Professional Made Easy & Ruby Programming Professional Made Easy

Table Of Contents

Introduction

I want to thank you and congratulate you for purchasing the book, "Professional C++ Programming Made Easy".

This book contains proven steps and strategies on how to learn the C++ programming language as well as its applications.

There's no need to be a professional developer to code quick and simple C++ programs. With this book, anyone with basic computer knowledge can explore and enjoy the power of the *C++ Programming Language*. Included are the following fundamental topics for any beginner to start coding *today:*

- The basic C++ terms

- Understanding the C++ Program Structure

- Working with Variables, Expressions, and Operators

- Using the Input and Output Stream for User Interaction

- Creating Logical Comparisons

- Creating Loops and Using Condition Statements

- And Many More!

Thanks again for purchasing this book, I hope you enjoy it!

Chapter 1 – Introduction to C++

What You Will Learn:

**A Brief History of the C++ Language

**C++ Basic Terminology

**C++ Program Structure

C++ is one of the most popular programming languages that people are using today. More specifically, C++ is a library of "commands" that tell your computer what to do and how to do it. These commands make up the C++ *source code*.

Take note that C++ is different from the *C* programming language that came before it. In fact, it is supposedly better version of the C language when *Bjarne Stroustrup* created it back in 1983.

Even today, the C++ language serves as the "starting point" for many experts in the world of programming. Although it is particularly easy to learn and apply, the ceiling for C++ mastery is incredibly high.

C++ Basic Terminology

Of course, the first step in learning the C++ programming language is to understand the basic terms. To prevent any unnecessary confusion at any point as you read this book, this section explains the most commonly used terms in the C++ program syntax. Just like the entire programming language itself, most terms in C++ are easy to remember and understand.

Compiler

Before anything else, take note that a compiler is needed to run the codes you've written with C++. Think of compilers as "translators" that convert programming language into *machine language* – the language that a computer understands. The machine language consists of only two characters (1s and 0s), which is why it is also called as *binary language*. If you're learning C++ at school, then you shouldn't worry about getting a compiler for C++ *or* an *Integrated Development Environment* for that matter.

Integrated Development Environment

An Integrated Development Environment (IDE) is essentially the software you're using to write C++ programs. It only makes sense for IDEs to come with compilers needed to run your codes. If you have no experience with C++ programming and attempting to learn it on your own, you can opt for a free C++ IDE such as *Code::Blocks*. A good choice for complete beginners is to opt for a simple C++ IDE such as *Quincy 2005* since there is very little setup required.

Variables and Parameters

Variables are individual blocks in the program's memory that contains a given value. A value may be set as a constant, determined by the value of other variables using operators, or set/changed through user input. Variables are denoted by variable names or *identifiers*. In programming with C++, you can use any variable name you desire as long as all characters are valid. Remember that only alphanumeric characters and "underscores" (_) can be used in identifiers. Punctuation marks and other symbols are not allowed.

Keep in mind that variables always need to be *declared* first before they can be used. Declaring variables are different from deciding their actual values; meaning both processes are done in two different codes. These processes will be explained in the next chapter.

"Parameters" work the same way as regular variables. In fact, they are even written in the same syntax. However, parameters and variables are initialized in different ways. Parameters are specifically included in *functions* to allow arguments to be passed to a separate location from which the functions are called.

7

Statements

Every program written with C++ consists of different lines of code that performs tasks such as setting variables, calling functions, and other expressions. These lines are *statements*. Each individual statement always ends with a semicolon (;). More importantly, statements in a function are executed chronologically based on which comes first. Of course, this order can be altered using *flow control statements* such as "if statements" and "loops".

Functions

Functions are blocks in a C++ program structured to complete a single task. You can call upon functions at any point whilst the program is running. Curly brackets or braces ({}) enclose the statements or "body" in each function. Aside from a function name, functions are also set with corresponding "types" which refer to the requested form of *returned value*. You can also use and set parameters at the beginning of each function. They are enclosed in parentheses "()" and separated using commas (,).

In C++, the following is the most used syntax when creating functions:

"type" "name" (parameter 1, parameter 2, parameter 3, ...)
{
        "statements";
}

Comments

When working on particularly bigger projects, most experienced programmers use "comments" that can be used as descriptions for specific sections in a C++ program. Comments are completely ignored by a compiler and can therefore ignore proper coding syntax. Comments are preceded either by a *two slashes* (//) or a *slash-asterisk* (/*). You will find comments in the examples throughout this book to help you understand them. A quick example would be the *"Hello World!"* program below. Of course, you can also use comments in your future projects for reference and debugging purposes.

Programming Box Set #59: C++ Programming Professional Made Easy & Ruby Programming Professional Made Easy

The C++ Program Structure

The program structure of C++ is very easy to understand. The compiler reads every line of code from top to bottom. This is why the first part of a C++ program usually starts with *preprocessor directives* and the declaration of variables and their values. The best way to illustrate this structure is to use the most popular example in the world of C++ -- the "Hello World!" program. Take note of the lines of code as well as the comments below:

#include <iostream> // this is a preprocessor directive

int main() // this line initiates the function named main, which should be found in every C++ program

{

> **std::cout << "Hello World!";** // the statements found between the curly braces make up the main function's body

> **return 0;** // the return 0; statement is required to tell the program that the function ran correctly. However, some compilers do not require this line in the main function

}

The topmost line ("#include <iostream>") is a preprocessor directive that defines a section of the standard C++ programming library known as the Input/Output Stream or simply *iostream*. This section handles the input and output operations in C++ programs. Remember that this is important if you wish to use "std::cout" in the main function's body.

The first line "int main ()" initializes the main function. Remember that the "int" refers to the *integer* data type and he "main" refers to the function's name. There are other data types aside from int. But you should focus on the integer data type for now. Since the "Hello World!" program does not need a parameter, it leaves the space between the parentheses succeeding the function name blank. Also, bear in mind that you should NOT place a semicolon (;) after initializing functions.

Next is the function's body, denoted by the open curly brace. This particular part ("std::cout") of the program refers to the **st**andard **c**haracter **out**put device, which is the computer's display device. Next comes the *insertion operator* (<<) from the input/output stream which means the rest of the line is to be outputted (excluding quotations). Lastly, the statement is closed with a semicolon (;).

The last line in the function's body is the *return statement* ("return = 0;"). Remember that the return expression (in this example, "0") depends on the data type specified upon initialization of the function. However, it is possible to create functions without the need for return statements using the "void" function type. For example; *void main ().*

An alternate way to do this is to include the line "using namespace std;" under the preprocessor line so you no longer need to write "std::" each time you use it. If you opt for this method, the code would look like:

#include <iostream>

using namespace std;

int main()

{

    cout << "Hello World!";

    return 0;

}

Chapter 2 – C++ Variables and Operators

What You Will Learn:

**Introduction to C++ Operators and How to Use Them*

**Declaring and Determining the Value of Variables*

**Creating New Lines in the Program Output*

In a C++ program, variables and constants are controlled or "operated" using *Operators*. Take note that the basic operators in the C++ programming language are essentially the same as arithmetic operator. This includes the equal sign (=) for assigning expressions, the plus sign (+) for addition, the minus sign (-) for subtraction, the asterisk (*) for multiplication, the forward slash (/) for division, and the percentage sign (%) for obtaining the remainder from any expression.

C++ also uses other operators to fulfill additional tasks other than basic arithmetic operations. As mentioned in the previous chapter, the iostream header allowed you to use the insertion operator (<<) for processing output. There are also different operators accessible even without the #include directive. These "basic" operators can be categorized under *increment/decrement operators, comparison operators, compound assignment operators,* and *logical operators.*

Declaring Variables

Before using variables in C++ operations, you must first declare them and determine their values. Again, declaring variables and giving their values are two separate processes. The syntax for declaring variables are as follows:

"type" "variable";

Just like when initializing functions, you need to specify the data type to be used for a given variable. For example; say you want to declare "x" as an integer variable. The initialization should look like this:

int x;

After the declaration of x, you can give it a value using the assign operator (=). For example; to assign the value "99" to variable x, use the following line:

x = 99;

Make sure to declare a variable first before you assign a value to it. Alternatively, you can declare a variable and assign a value to it using a single line. This can be done using:

int x = 99;

Aside from setting these expressions as you write the program, you can also use operations and user input to determine their values as the program runs. But first, you need to learn about the other operators in C++.

Increment and Decrement Operators

The increment operator consists of two plus signs (++) while the decrement operator consists of two minus signs (--). The main purpose of increment and decrement operators is to shorten the expression of adding and subtracting 1 from any given variable. For example; if x = 2, then ++x should equal 3 while −x should equal 1.

If being used to determine the values of two or more variables, increment and decrement operators can be included as either a prefix or suffix. When used as a suffix (x++ or x--), it denotes the original value of x *before* adding or subtracting 1. When run on their own, both ++x and x++ have the same meaning. But when used in setting other variables, the difference is made obvious. Here is a simple example to illustrate the difference:

X = 5;

Y = ++x;

In this example, the value of y is determined *after* increasing the value of x. In other words, the value of y in this example is equal to 6.

X = 5;

Y = x++;

In this example, the value of y is determined *before* increasing the value of x. In other words, the value of y in this example is equal to 6.

Compound Assignment Operators

Aside from basic arithmetic operators and the standard assignment operator (=), compound assignment operators can also be used to perform an operation before a value is assigned. Compound assignment operators are basically shortened versions of normal expressions that use basic arithmetic operators.

Here are some examples of compound assignment operators:

x -= 1; // this is the same as the expression x = x − 1;

x *= y; // this is the same as the expression x = x * y;

x += 1;   // this is the same as the expression x = x + 1;

x /= y;   // this is the same as the expression x = x / y;

Comparison Operators

Variables and other expressions can be compared using relational or comparison operators. These operators are used to check whether a value is greater than, less than, or equal to another. Here are the comparison operators used in C++ and their description:

== - checks if the values are equal

< - checks if the first value is less than the second

> - checks if the first value is greater than the second

<=   -   checks if the first value is less than *or* equal to the second

>=   -   checks if the first value is greater than *or* equal to the second

!=   -   checks if the values are NOT equal

Comparison operators are commonly used in creating condition statements. They can also be used to evaluate an expression and return a *Boolean value* ("true" or "false"). Using the comparison operators listed above; here are some example expressions and their corresponding Boolean value:

(8 == 1) // this line evaluates to "false"

(8 > 1) // this line evaluates to "true"

(8 != 1) // this line evaluates to "true"

(8 <= 1) // this line evaluates to "false"

Also take note that the Boolean value "false" is equivalent to "0" while "true" is equivalent to other non-zero integers.

Aside from numerical values, the value of variables can also be checked when using comparison operators. Simply use a variable's identifier when creating the expression. Of course, the variable must be declared and given an identified value first before a valid comparison can be made. Here is an example scenario

```
#include <iostream>
using namespace std;

int main ()

{
        int a = 3;    // the values of a and b are set first
        int b = 4;
        cout << "Comparison a < b = " << (a < b);
        return 0;
}
```

The output for this code is as follows:

Comparison a < b = true

Take note that the insertion operator (<<) is used to insert the value of the expression "a < b" in the output statement, which is denoted in the 7th line ("cout << "Comparison a < b = "...). Don't forget that you *need an output statement* in order to see if your code works. The following code will produce no errors, but it won't produce an output either:

#include <iostream>

int main (

{

    int a = 3;
    int b = 4;
    (a < b);
    return 0;

}

In this code, it is also true that a < b. However, no output will be produced since the lines necessary for the program output are omitted.

Logical Operators

There are also other logical operators in C++ that can determine the values of Boolean data. They are the NOT (!), AND (&&), and OR (||) operators. Here are specific examples on how they are used:

!(6 > 2)　　// the **NOT** operator (!) completely reverses any relational expressions and produces the opposite result. This expression is false because 6 > 2 is correct

(6 > 2 && 5 < 10) // the **AND** (&&) operator only produces true if both expressions correct. This expression is true because both 6 > 2 && 5 < 10 are correct

(6 = 2 || 5 < 10) // the **OR** (||) operator produces true if one of the expressions are correct. This expression is true because the 5 < 10 is correct although 6 = 2 is false.

You can also use the NOT operator in addition to the other two logical operators. For example:

!(6 = 2 || 5 < 10) // this expression is false

!(6 > 2 && 5 < 10) // this expression is also false

!(6 < 2 && 5 < 10) // this expression is true

Creating New Lines

From this point on in this book, you will be introduced to simple C++ programs that produce output with multiple lines. To create new lines when producing output, all you need to do is to use the *new line character* (\n). Alternatively, you can use the "endl;" manipulator to create new lines when using the "cout" code. The main difference is that the *internal buffer* for the output stream is "flushed" whenever you use the "endl;" manipulator with "cout". Here are examples on how to use both:

cout << "Sentence number one \nSentence number two";

The example above uses the new line character.

cout << "Sentence number one" << endl;
cout << "Sentence number two";

The example above uses "endl;".

Of course, the first code (using \n) is relatively simpler and easier for general output purposes. Both will produce the following output:

Sentence number one

Sentence number two

Chapter 3 – All About User Input

What You Will Learn:

**Utilizing the Input Stream

**Using Input to Determine or Modify Values

**How to Input and Output Strings

Up to this point, you've learned how to make a C++ program that can perform arithmetic operations, comparisons, and can produce output as well. This time, you will learn how to code one of the most important aspects of computer programs – *user input*.

As stated earlier, user input can be utilized to determine or modify the values of certain variables. C++ programs use abstractions known as *streams* to handle input and output. Since you already know about the syntax for output ("cout"), it's time to learn about the syntax for input ("cin").

The Extraction Operator

The input syntax "cin" is used with the *extraction operator* (>>) for formatted input. This combination along with the *keyboard* is the standard input for most program environments. Remember that you still need to declare a variable first before input can be made. Here is a simple example:

int x; // this line declares the variable identifier x. Take note of the data type "int" which means that only an integer value is accepted

cin >> x;   // this line extracts input from the cin syntax and stores it to x

User input can also be requested for multiple variables in a single line. For example; say you want to store integer values for variables x and y. This should look like:

int x, y;   // this line declares the two variables

cin >> x >> y;   // this line extracts user input for variables x and y

Take note that the program will automatically require the user to input *two* values for the two variables. Which comes first depends on the order of the variables in the line (in this case, input for variable "x" is requested first).

Here is an example of a program that extracts user input and produces an output:

#include <iostream>   // again, this is essential for input and output
using namespace std;

int main ()

{

    int x;
    cout << "Insert a random number \n";
    cin >> x;   // this is where user input is extracted
    cout << "You inserted: " << x;
    return 0;

}

Bear in mind that the value extracted from the input stream overwrites any initial value of a variable. For example, if the variable was declared as "int x = 2;" but was later followed by the statement "cin >> x;", the new value will then replace the original value until the program/function restarts or if an assignment statement is introduced.

Strings

Keep in mind that there are other types you can assign to variables in C++. Aside from integers, another fundamental type is the *string*. A string is basically a variable type that can store sets of characters in a specific sequence. In other words, this is how you can assign words or sentences as values for certain variables.

First of all, you need to add the preprocessor directive "#include <string>" before you can use strings in your program. Next, you need to declare a string before it can receive assignments. For example; if you want to declare a string for "Name" and assign a value for it, you can use the code:

#include <string>
using namespace std;

int main ()

{

  string name;
  name = "Insert your name here"; // including quotations

}

Creating output using strings is basically the same as with integers. You only need to use "cout" and insert the string to the line. The correct syntax is as follows:

string name;

Name = "Your Name Here";

cout << "My name is: " << name;

Without any changes, the output for the above code is:

Your Name Here

Inputting Strings

To allow user input values for strings, you need to use the function "getline" in addition to the standard input stream "cin". The syntax for this is "getline (cin, [string]);". Below is an example program that puts string input into application.

```
#include <iostream>
#include <string>
using namespace std;

int main ()

{
        string name;
        cout << "Greetings! What is your name?\n";
        getline (cin, name); // this is the extraction syntax
        cout << "Welcome " << name;
        return 0;

}
```

Take note that strings have "blank" values by default. This means nothing will be printed if no value is assigned or if there is no user input.

Chapter 4 – Using Flow Control Statements

What You Will Learn:

**If and Else Selection Statements

**Creating Choices

**Creating Iterating/Looping Statements

Remember that statements are the basic building blocks of a program written using C++. Each and every line that contains expressions such as a variable declaration, an operation, or an input extraction is a statement.

However, these statements are *linear* without some form of flow control that can establish the "sense" or "logic" behind a C++ program. This is why you should learn how to utilize flow control statements such as *selection statements* and *looping statements*.

If and Else Statements

If and else statements are the most basic form of logic in a C++ program. Basically, the main purpose of an "if" statement is to allow the execution of a specific line or "block" of multiple statements only *if* a specified condition is fulfilled.

Next is the "else" statement which allows you to specify what would occur in case the conditions aren't met. Without an "else" statement, everything inside the "if" statement will be completely ignored. Here the syntax for an "if" and "else" statement:

if (age >= 18)
        cout << "You are allowed to drink.";

else

      cout << "You are not yet allowed to drink.";

Remember that conditions can only be set using comparison operators and logical operators (refer to Chapter 2). Take note that you can also execute multiple statements using if/else conditions by enclosing the lines in curly braces. It is also possible to use composite conditions using logical operators such as AND (&&) and OR (||).

Finally, you can use another "if" statement after an "else" statement for even more possibilities. Of course, you also need to specify conditions for every "if" statement you use. Here is a good example that demonstrates what you can do using "if" and "else" statements in addition to user input:

```
#include <iostream>
using namespace std;

int main()

{
    int number;
    cout << "Enter a number from 1-3\n";
    cin >> number;
    if (number == 1 || number == 2)
        cout << "You have entered either 1 or 2.";
    else if (number == 3)
        cout << "You have entered 3.";
    else
    {
        cout << "Please follow the instructions\n";
        cout << "Please Try Again.";
    }
    return 0;
}
```

There are 3 possible outcomes in the program above. The first outcome is achieved if the user entered any of the numbers 1 or 2. The second outcome is achieved if the user entered the number 3. Lastly, the third outcome is achieved if the user entered a different number other the ones specified.

Creating Choices (Yes or No)

Another way to utilize if/else statements is to create "Yes or No" choices. For this, you need to make use of the variable type "char" which can hold a character from the *8-bit character set* (you can use char16_t, char32_t, or wchar_t for larger character sets; but this is not usually necessary). Just like all other variables, a "char" variable needs to be declared before it can be used.

Of course, you want the user to make the choice, which is why you need to use the "cin" function to extract user input. Here is a simple program that asks for the user's gender:

```
#include <iostream>
using namespace std;

int main()
{
        char gender; // this is the char variable declaration
        cout << "Male or Female? (M/F)";
        cin >> gender; // user input is stored to gender
        if (gender == 'm' || gender == 'M')
                cout << "You have selected Male.";
        else if (gender == 'f' || gender == 'F')
                cout << "You have selected Female.";
        else
                cout << "Please follow the instructions.";
        return 0;

}
```

Take note that you should use *single quotation marks* (') when pinpointing "char" values. In C++, "char" values are always called inside single quotation marks. Additionally, remember that "char" values are case-sensitive, which is why the example above used the OR (||) operator in the conditions to accept both lowercase and uppercase answers. You can see that the program above checked if the user entered 'm', 'M', 'f', or 'F'.

Looping Statements

Lastly, using "loops" allow statements to be executed for a set number of times or until a condition is met. By incorporating other statements in loops, you can do far more than just create pointless repetitions. But first, you need to be familiar with the different types of loops.

There are 3 types of loops in C++ -- *while, do,* and *for.*

While Loop

The "*while loop*" is regarded as the simplest form of loop in the C++. Basically, it repeats the statement(s) as long as the given condition is true. Keep in mind that your code should be structured to eventually fulfill the condition; otherwise you might create an "infinite loop".

Here is an example of a while loop:

int x = 100;

```
while (x >= 0)      // the condition for the loop is set
    {
    cout << x;
    --x;    // the value of x is decreased
    }
```

In this example, the loop executes as long as the value of x is greater than or equal to 0. Take note of the decrement operator (--) in the statement "--x;". This makes sure that the value of x is continually decreased until the condition is met and the loop ends.

Do-While Loop

The next type of loop is the *"do-while loop"*. The do-while loop is essentially the same as the while loop. The main difference is that the do-while loop allows the execution of the statement(s) at least *once* before the condition is checked. Whereas in the while loop, the condition is checked *first*.

Here is an example of a do-while loop:

```
int x = 100;
int y;

do
     {
     cout << "The value is " << x << "\n";
     cout << "Enter a value to subtract.";
     cin >> y;
     x -= y;
     }
while (x > 0);      // in the do-while loop, the condition is checked last
```

In the example above, the statements are executed at least once before the value of x is checked. Whereas in a while loop, there is a possibility that the statement(s) will not be executed at all.

For Loop

The third type of loop is the *"for loop"* which has specific areas for the *initialization, condition,* and *increase*. These three sections are sequentially executed throughout the life cycle of the loop. By structure, for loops are created to run a certain number of times because increment or decrement operators are usually used in the "increase" section.

Here is the syntax for this loop to help you understand it better:

for (int x = 10; x > 0; x--)

Notice the three expressions inside the parentheses (int x = 10; x > 0; x--) are separated in semicolons. These parameters denote the three sections of the loop. You may also use multiple expressions for each section using a comma (,). Here is the syntax for this:

```
for ( int x = 10, y = 0; x != y; --x, ++y )
    {
    cout << "X and Y is different\n";
    }
```

In this example, the loop is executed as long as x is not equal to y. And in order for the loop to end, the values of x and y are adjusted until the value of x equals the value of y. Based on the parameters above, the statement "X and Y is different" will run a total of 5 times before the loop is ended.

Conclusion

Thank you again for purchasing this book!

I hope this book was able to help you to learn and understand the C++
programming language!

The next step is to start from where you are now and try to learn something new.
Keep in mind that you've only scratched the surface of all the things you can do in
the world of C++!

Finally, if you enjoyed this book, please take the time to share your thoughts and
post a review on Amazon. We do our best to reach out to readers and provide the
best value we can. Your positive review will help us achieve that. It'd be greatly
appreciated!

Thank you and good luck!

Book 2
Ruby Programming
Professional Made Easy
BY SAM KEY

Expert Ruby Programming Language Success in a Day for any Computer User

Programming Box Set #59: C++ Programming Professional Made Easy & Ruby Programming Professional Made Easy

Table Of Contents

Introduction

I want to thank you and congratulate you for purchasing the book, *"Professional Ruby Programming Made Easy: Expert Ruby Programming Language Success in a Day for Any Computer User!"*

This book contains proven steps and strategies on how to write basic lines of code in Ruby. This is especially made for amateur programmers with little to no experience in coding.

Ruby is a programming language which people think is ideal for newbies in the programming field. Congratulations on choosing this programming language. In this book, you will be introduced to all the fundamental aspects of coding in Ruby.

This book will give you a huge boost in your programming skills. However, it is also important to quickly supplement yourself with advanced Ruby tutorials after you are done with this book to retain the knowledge you gain from it.

Thanks again for purchasing this book, I hope you enjoy it!

Chapter 1: Setting Up

This book will assume that you are a bit familiar with computer programming and have made a few lines of codes in some languages. Also, from time to time, the book will provide further explanation of terms and methods that can easily confuse new programmers. In case you encounter a foreign term in the discussion, just take note of it since it and other such terms will be discussed later.

Before anything else, get the latest stable version of Ruby from the web. As of this writing, Ruby's stable version is 2.1.5.

Go to https://www.ruby-lang.org/en/documentation/installation/. In there, you can get the right installer package for the operating system that your computer is running on.

Be mindful of what you are going to download. Many people tend to download the source code of Ruby instead of the installation packages.

Take note of the location or directory where you will install Ruby. Once you are done with the installation, open Ruby's interactive shell.

For people who are using a computer running on Windows, you will find the interactive interpreter inside the bin folder located inside your Ruby installation folder. The file is named irb.bat. If you have installed Ruby using the default location, the interactive shell will be located at: "c:\Ruby21\bin\irb.bat".

What is the interactive shell anyway? In Ruby, you can program using two modes: the interactive mode and the programming mode.

Ruby's Interactive Mode

The interactive mode is an environment wherein Ruby will provide immediate feedback in every line of code or statement you type in to it. It is an ideal environment where new Ruby programmers can test and experiment with codes quickly. You will be using this mode in most parts of this book.

The interactive mode or shell will appear like a typical console or command prompt. In the shell, you should be familiar with two things. First is the cursor. Second is the prompt.

The cursor indicates where you can type or if you can type anything. In the interpreter shell, you can use overtype mode on this by pressing the insert key on your keyboard. You can return to insert mode by pressing the insert key again.

The prompt will look like this: irb(main):001:0>. If this prompt is on, it means that Ruby is ready to accept a line of code or statement from you. For now, type a letter a in the prompt and press the Enter key. The shell or interpreter will move the cursor, show a bunch of text, and display the prompt once again:

irb(main):001:0> a
NameError: undefined local variable or method 'a' for main:Object
    from (irb):1
    from C:/Ruby21/bin/irb:11:in '<main>'
irb(main):002:0>

This time, type "a" on the shell and then press the Enter key. Instead of an error, you have received => "a". Now, type "1" without the quotes. Just like before, the interpreter just provided you with a reply containing the number you entered.

Why does the letter a without the quotes returned an error? As you can see, Ruby provided you with an error message when you just entered the letter a without quotes. In Ruby, characters enclosed in double or single quotes are treated differently.

In the case of the letter a, Ruby understood that when you input "a" with the quotes, you meant that you are inputting the letter a. On the other hand, Ruby thought of something else when you input the letter a without the quotes, which will be discussed later.

You will receive error messages like the one before or other variations of it if you input something that violates Ruby's syntax or something that is impossible to be evaluated or executed by the interpreter. In simple terms, Ruby will provide you notifications like that if it does not understand what you said or cannot do what you commanded.

Now, type "1 + 1", without the double quotes, and press the Enter key. Instead of an error, you will receive this instead:

=> 2

Every time you press the Enter key, the shell check the command or statement you created. If it does not violate the syntax, it will proceed on checking if every word and symbols you placed make sense. Once the statement passes that check, it will evaluate and execute the statement and provide a result or feedback.

In this case, Ruby has evaluated the addition operation you commanded and replied the number 2, which is the sum of 1 + 1. Just before the number 2, an equal sign and "greater than" sign were placed. Those two denotes that the next value is the result of the statement you entered.

You might have thought that Ruby can be a good calculator. Indeed it is, but statements like "1 + 1" and "a" are only processed like that in the interactive mode of Ruby. If you include a line like that when coding in programming mode, you will certainly encounter a syntax error.

Ruby's Programming Mode

On the other hand, the programming mode is a method wherein you can execute blocks of code in one go. You will need to type the code of your program first before you can run and see what it will do.

You will need a text editor to type your program. Any simple text editor such as Notepad in Windows is sufficient for programming Ruby. However, to reduce typos and keyword mistakes, it is advisable that you use a source code editor, which will provide you with syntax highlighting and checking. In Windows users, a few of the best source code editors you can use for Ruby programming are Notepad++, TextWrangler, JEdit, and Crimson Editor.

Once you are done typing your code, save it as a .rb file. For Windows users: if you have let Ruby associate .rb and .rbw files to it, all .rb files or Ruby code you have created can be opened by just double clicking on them. They will act as if they are typical Windows program.

By the way, programming mode does not provide instant reply to your expressions. For example, if you input a = 1 + 1 in interactive mode, it will reply with => 2. In programming mode, that statement will not provide any output.

Also, if one of the lines encounters an error, the program will stop executing the next lines after the line that generated the error.

Chapter 2: Ruby Syntax

In the first chapter, you have encountered your first syntax error. For those who are not familiar with the term syntax, syntax is a set of 'language' rules that you must follow in order for a programming language (in this case, Ruby) to understand you.

A programming language's syntax is similar to English grammar where you need to correctly arrange parts of the sentence—such as verbs, nouns, and adjectives—to make it coherent and grammatically correct.

The two major differences between Ruby's syntax (or other programming languages' syntax as well) and English's set of grammar rules are Ruby's syntax's strictness and inflexibility. It is set to behave like that because computers, unlike humans, cannot understand or comprehend context. Also, if computers understand context and programming languages' syntaxes become lax, computer programming will become difficult.

First, computer will become prone to misunderstanding or misinterpreting your statements. If you point to a jar of jam in a shelf full of jars and requested people to get the one you want, most of them will surely get and give you the wrong jar. That kind of situation will happen if a programming language's syntax became loose.

Here are some of Ruby's syntax rules:

Whitespace

Whitespace (continuous spaces and tabs) are ignored in Ruby code unless they are placed inside strings. For example, the expression "1 + 1", "1 + 1", or 1+1 will provide the same result in Ruby.

Line Ending Terminators

New lines and semicolons are treated as line endings. Ruby works by reading your program's lines one by one. Each line is considered a statement. A statement is a combination of keywords, operators, values, methods, and properties, which is translated as a command.

Every time you put a semicolon or move to the next line, the previous line will be treated as a statement. There are some cases that if you do not place a semicolon but used a new line character (the one that the Enter key produces and pushes the cursor to move to the next line) to write a new line of code will make Ruby think that the previous line and the new line of code is just one statement. For example:

irb(main):001:0> 1 +
irb(main):002:0* 1 +
irb(main):003:0*

If you typed that in Ruby's interactive mode, you will not encounter an error or reply from Ruby. Instead, it allowed you to move on to the next line and type another line of code.

If you have noticed, the greater than sign at the end of the prompt changed into an asterisk. The asterisk denotes that all the succeeding lines of code after the previous one will be treated as one statement in Ruby or the next lines are meant to be continuations of the previous line.

Ruby behaved like that since you left an operator at the end of the line and did not place a value on the operator's right hand side. So, Ruby is treating the example as 1 + 1 +. If you place another 1 at the last line, Ruby will interpret that 1 as the last value to your expression and evaluate it. It will then produce a reply, which is => 3.

Case Sensitivity

Identifiers or names of constants, variables, and methods in Ruby are case sensitive. For example, a variable named Variable1 is different from variable1.

Comments

In computer languages, comments are used to serve as markers, reminders, or explanations within the program. Comments are ignored by Ruby and are not executed like regular statements.

Some convert statements in order to disable them. It is handy during debugging or testing alternate statements to get what they want since deleting a statement may make them forget it after a few minutes of coding another line.

To create comments in Ruby, use the hash sign (#) to let Ruby know that the succeeding characters is a comment line. You can insert comments at the end of statements. For example:

irb(main):001:0> #This is a comment.
irb(main):002:0* 1 + 1
=> 2
irb(main):003:0> 1 + 1 #This is a comment.
=> 2

irb(main):003:0>

As you can see, the line after the hash sign was just ignored and Ruby just evaluated the expression 1 + 1.

In case you are going to start programming using Ruby's programming mode, there will be times that you will want to create multiple lines of comments. You can still use hash signs to create multiple lines. For example:

#This is a comment.
#This is another comment.
#This is the last comment.

If you do not want to use that method, you can do this by using the =begin and =end keyword. Below is an example on how to use them:

=begin
This is a comment
This is another comment.
This is the last comment.
=end

All lines after the =begin and before the =end keyword will be treated as comment lines.

Those are just the primary rules in Ruby's syntax. Some commands have syntax of their own. They will be discussed together with the commands themselves.

Chapter 3: Parts of a Statement

You have been seeing the term statement in the previous chapters. As mentioned before, a statement is a combination of keywords, operators, variables, constants, values, expressions, methods, and properties which is translated as a command.

In this chapter, you will know what six of those parts are: variables, constants, keywords, values, operators, and expressions. Let's start with variables.

Variables

In Math, you know that variables are placeholders for values. For example:

x = 1 + 1

x = 2

y = 3

In the previous line, variable x has a value of 2 and variable y has a value of 3. Variables in Ruby (or other programming languages) act the same way – as placeholders. However, unlike in Math, variables in Ruby do not act as placeholders for numbers alone. It can contain different types of values like strings and objects.

To create variables in Ruby, all you need is to assign a value to one. For example:

irb(main):001:0> a = 12

That example commands Ruby to create a variable named a and assign the number 12 as its value. To check the value of a variable in Ruby's interpreter mode, input a on a new line and press the Enter key. It will produce the result:

=> 12

A while ago, instead of getting a reply like that from Ruby, you have got this instead:

NameError: undefined local variable or method 'a' for main:Object
**   from (irb):1**
**   from C:/Ruby21/bin/irb:11:in '<main>'**

Technically, the error means that Ruby was not able to find a variable or method with the name a. Now, when you input a, it does not produce that error anymore since you have already created a variable named a.

By the name, in computer programming, the names you give to variables and other entities in the program are called identifiers. Some call them IDs or tokens instead.

There are some set of rules when giving an identifier to a variable. Identifiers can contain letters, numbers, and underscores. A variable identifier must start with a lower case letter or an underscore. It may also contain one or more characters. Also, variable identifiers should not be the same with a keyword or reserved words.

Just like any programming languages, reserved or special keywords cannot be used as identifiers.

Constants

Constants are like variables, but you can only assign a value to them once in your program and their identifiers must start with an uppercase letter. Reassigning a value to them will generate an error or a warning.

Keywords

Keywords are special reserved words in Ruby that perform specific functions and commands. Some of them are placeholder for special values such as true, false, and nil.

The nil value means that the entity that contains it does not have a value. To put it simply, all variables will have the nil value if no value was assigned to it. When they are used and they have nil as their value, Ruby will return a warning if the – w is on.

Values

In Ruby, there are multiple types of values that you can assign in a variable. In programming, they are called literals. In coding Ruby, you will be dealing with these literals every time.

Integers

You can write integers in four forms or numeral systems: decimal, hexadecimal, octal, and binary. To make Ruby understand that you are declaring integers in hexadecimal (base 16), octal (base 8), or binary (base 2), you should use prefixes or leading signs.

If you are going to use octal, use 0 (zero). If you are going to use hexadecimal, use 0x (zero-x). If you are going to use binary, use 0b (zero-b). If you are going to use decimal, there is no need for any optional leading signs.

Depending on the size of the integer, it can be categorized in the class Fixnum or Bignum.

Floating Numbers

Any integer with decimals is considered a floating number. All floating numbers are under the class Float.

Strings

Strings are values inside single or double quotation marks. They are treated as text in Ruby. You can place expression evaluation inside strings without terminating your quotes. You can just insert expressions by using the hash sign and enclosing the expression using curly braces. For example:

irb(main):001:0> a = "the sum of 3 and 1 is: #{3 + 1}."
=> "the sum of 3 and 1 is: 4."

You can also access variables or constants in Ruby and include them in a string by placing a hash sign (#) before the variable or constant's name. For example:

irb(main):001:0> b = "string inside variable."
=> "string inside variable."
irb(main):002:0> b = "You can access a #{b}"
=> "You can access a string inside variable."

Arrays

An array is a data type that can contain multiple data or values. Creating arrays in Ruby is simple. Type Array and then follow it with values enclosed inside square brackets. Make sure that you separate each value with a comma. Any exceeding commas will be ignored and will not generate error. For example:

irb(main):001:0> arraysample = Array[1, 2, 3]
=> [1, 2, 3]

To access a value of an array, you must use its index. The index of an array value depends on its location in the array. For example, the value 2 in the arraysample variable has an index number of 0. The value 2, has an index of 1. And the value 3, has an index of 2. The index increments by 1 and starts with zero.

Below is an example on how to access a value in an array:

irb(main):001:0> arraysample[2]
=> 3

Hashes or Associative Arrays:

Hashes are arrays that contain paired keys (named index) and values. Instead of a numbered index, you can assign and use keys to access your array values.

irb(main):001:0> hashsample = Hash["First" => 1, "Second" = > 2]
=> {"First"=>1, "Second"=>2}

To access a hash value, you just need to call it using its key instead of an index number. For example:

irb(main):001:0> hashsample["Second"]
=> 2

Expressions

Expressions are combinations of operators, variables, values, and/or keywords. Expressions result into a value or can be evaluated by Ruby. A good example of an expression is 1 + 1. In that, Ruby can evaluate that expression and it will result to 2. The plus sign (+) is one of many operators in Ruby.

You can assign expression to a variable. The result of the expression will be stored on the variable instead of the expression itself. For example:

irb(main):001:0> a = 1 + 1
=> 2

If you check the value of a by inputting a into the shell, it will return 2 not 1 + 1.

As mentioned a while ago, expressions can also contain variables. If you assign a simple or complex expression with a variable to another variable, Ruby will handle all the evaluation. For example:

irb(main):001:0> a = 2
=> 2
irb(main):002:0> b = 4
=> 4
irb(main):003:0> c = a + b + 6
=> 12

Operators

Operators are symbols or keywords that command the computer to perform operations or evaluations. Ruby's operators are not limited to performing arithmetic operations alone. The following are the operators you can use in Ruby:

Arithmetic Operators

Arithmetic operators allow Ruby to evaluate simple Math expressions. They are: + for addition, - for subtraction, * for multiplication, / for division, % for modulus, and ** for exponent.

Division in Ruby works differently. If you are dividing integers, you will get an integer quotient. If the quotient should have a fractional component or decimal on it, they will be removed. For example:

irb(main):001:0> 5 / 2
=> 2

If you want to get an accurate quotient with a fractional component, you must perform division with fractional components For example:

irb(main):001:0> 5.0 / 2
=> 2.5

For those who are unfamiliar with modulus: modulus performs regular division and returns the remainder instead of the quotient. For example:

irb(main):001:0> 5 % 2
=> 1

Comparison Operators

Ruby can compare numbers, too, with the help of comparison operators. Comparison operations provide two results only: true or false. For example:

irb(main):001:0> 1 > 2
=> false

The value 1 is less than 2, but not greater than; therefore, Ruby evaluated that the expression is false.

Other comparison operators that you can use in Ruby are: == for has equal value, != for does not have equal value, > for greater than, < for less than, >= for greater than or equal, and <= for less than or equal. There four other comparison operators (===, <=>, .eql?, and .equal?) in Ruby, but you do not need them for now.

Assignment Operators

Assignment operators are used to assign value to operators, properties, and other entities in Ruby. You have already encountered the most used assignment operator, which is the equal sign (=). There are other assignment operators other than that, which are simple combination of the assignment operator (=) and arithmetic operators.

They are += for add and assign, -= for subtract and assign, *= for multiply and assign, /= for divide and assign, % for modulus and assign, and ** for raise and assign.

All of them perform the arithmetic operation and the values they use are the value of the entity on their left and the expression on their right first before assigning the result of the operation to the entity on its left. It might seem confusing, so here is an example:

```
irb(main):001:0> a = 1
=> 1
irb(main):002:0> a += 2
=> 3
```

In the example, variable a was given a value of 1. On the next statement, the add
and assign operator was used. After the operation, a's value became 3 because a +
2 = 3. That can also be achieved by doing this:

```
irb(main):001:0> a = 1
=> 1
irb(main):002:0> a = a + 2
=> 3
```

If the value to the right of these operators is an expression that contain multiple
values and operators, it will be evaluated first before the assignment operators
perform their operations. For example:

```
irb(main):001:0> a = 1
=> 1
irb(main):002:0> a += 3 * 2
=> 7
```

The expression 3 * 2 was evaluated first, which resulted to 6. Then six was added
to variable a that had a value of 1, which resulted to 7. And that value value was
assigned to variable a.

Other Operators

As you advance your Ruby programming skills, you will encounter more
operators. And they are:

> Logical Operator: and, or, &&, ||, !, not
> Defined Operator: defined?
> Reference Operators: ., ::

Chapter 4: Object Oriented Programming

In the previous chapters, you have learned the basics of Ruby programming. Those chapters also serve as your introduction to computer programming since most programming languages follow the same concepts and have similar entities in them. In this chapter, you will learn why some programmers love Ruby.

Ruby is an Object Oriented Programming (OOP) language. Object oriented programming makes use of objects and classes. Those objects and classes can be reused which in turn makes it easier to code programs that require multiple instances of values that are related to each other.

Programming methods can be categorized into two: Procedural and Object Oriented. If you have experienced basic programming before, you mostly have experienced procedural instead of object oriented.

In procedural, your program's code revolves around actions. For example, you have a program that prints what a user will input. It is probable that your program's structure will be as simple as take user input, assign the input to a variable, and then print the content of the variable. As you can see, procedural is a straightforward forward method.

Classes and Objects

Classes are like templates for objects. For example, a Fender Telecaster and a Gibson Les Paul are objects and they are under the electric guitar class.

In programming, you can call those guitars as instances of the class of objects named electric guitars. Each object has its own properties or characteristics.

Objects under the same class have same properties, but the value of those properties may differ or be the same per object. For example, think that an electric guitar's properties are: brand, number of strings, and number of guitar pickups.

Aside from that, each object has its own functions or things that it can do. When it comes to guitars, you can strum all the strings or you can just pick on one string.

If you convert that to Ruby code, that will appear as:

```
class ElectricGuitar
    def initialize
        @brand = "Local"
        @strings = 6
        @pickups = 3
    end
    def strum
```

```
            #Insert statements to execute when strum is called
     end
     def pick
            #Insert statements to execute when strum is called
end
```

Creating a Class

To create a class, you need to use the class keyword and an identifier. Class identifiers have the same syntax rules for constant identifiers. To end the creation of the class, you need to use the end keyword. For example:

```
irb(main):001:0> class Guitar
irb(main):002:1> end
=> nil
```

Creating an Object

Now, you have a class. It is time for you to create an object. To create one, all you need is to think of an identifier and assign the class name and the keyword new to it for it to become an object under a class. For example:

```
irb(main):001:0> fender = Guitar. new
=> #<Guitar:0x1234567>
```

Note: Do not forget to add a dot operator after the class name.

Unfortunately, the class Guitar does not contain anything in it. That object is still useless and cannot be used for anything. To make it useful, you need to add some methods and properties to it.

Methods

This is where it gets interesting. Methods allow your objects to have 'commands' of some sort. In case you want to have multiple lines of statements to be done, placing them under a class method is the best way to do that. To give your classes or objects methods, you will need to use the def (define) keyword. Below is an example:

```
irb(main):001:0> class Guitar
irb(main):002:1> def strum
irb(main):003:2> puts "Starts strumming."
irb(main):004:2> puts "Strumming."
irb(main):005:2> puts "Ends strumming."
irb(main):006:2> end
irb(main):007:1> end
=> :strum
```

Now, create a new object under that class.

irb(main):008:0> gibson = Guitar. new
=> #<Guitar:0x1234567>

To use the method you have created, all you need is to invoke it using the object. For example:

irb(main):009:0> gibson.strum
Starts strumming.
Strumming.
Ends strumming.
=> nil

By using the dot operator, you were able to invoke the method inside the gibson object under the Guitar class. All the objects that will be under Guitar class will be able to use that method.

Conclusion

Thank you again for purchasing this book!

I hope this book was able to help you understand how coding in Ruby works.

The next step is to:

- Learn more about flow control tools in Ruby

- Study about the other operators discussed in this book

- Research on how variables inside classes and objects work

Finally, if you enjoyed this book, please take the time to share your thoughts and post a review on Amazon. We do our best to reach out to readers and provide the best value we can. Your positive review will help us achieve that. It'd be greatly appreciated!

Thank you and good luck!

Check Out My Other Books

Below you'll find some of my other popular books that are popular on Amazon and Kindle as well. Simply click on the links below to check them out. Alternatively, you can visit my author page on Amazon to see other work done by me.

C Programming Success in a Day

Python Programming Success in a Day

PHP Programming Professional Made Easy

HTML Professional Programming Made Easy

CSS Programming Professional Made Easy

Windows 8 Tips for Beginners

C Programming Professional Made Easy

JavaScript Programming Made Easy

Rails Programming Professional Made Easy

C ++ Programming Success in a Day

If the links do not work, for whatever reason, you can simply search for these titles on the Amazon website to find them.